FOLDING TABLE NAPKINS

By Marianne
von Bornstedt and
Ulla Prytz

Sterling Publishing Co., Inc.   New York

Translated by Kenneth T. Dutfield
Adapted by Anne E. Kallem
Photographs by Olle Akerström
Cover photographs by Mats Nicklasson

Originally published by ICA Förlaget, Sweden, © 1968, under the title "Dukning och Servettbrytning."

Copyright © 1972 by Sterling Publishing Co., Inc.
Two Park Avenue, New York, N.Y. 10016
Distributed in Australia by Oak Tree Press Co., Ltd.
P.O. Box K514 Haymarket, Sydney 2000, N.S.W.
Distributed in the United Kingdom by Blandford Press
Link House, West Street, Poole, Dorset BH15 1LL, England
Distributed in Canada by Oak Tree Press Ltd.
% Canadian Manda Group, 215 Lakeshore Boulevard East
Toronto, Ontario M5A 3W9
Manufactured in the United States of America
All rights reserved
Library of Congress Catalog Card No.: 72-81040
Sterling ISBN 0-8069-5218-0 Trade
5219-9 Library
8974-2 Paper

Contents

Finess Pappers AB has supplied paper napkins, paper tablecloths, and
original drawings showing ways of folding napkins. Liljeholmens
Stearinfabriks AB, candles. AB Akerlund & Rausing, paper plates
and cups. AB Nordiska Kompaniet & AB Aveny Kristall, china,
glass and cutlery.

Before You Begin

Attractively folded table napkins can give even the plainest table setting or the most casual get-together for coffee a party look. Even if you are one of those people who despair, "I can't do anything clever with my hands," just try one or two projects—and watch that sleepyhead at break-fast or *the* important guest at dinner sit up and take notice.

Don't be put off by the complicated appearance of some of the napkins in this book. They are *all* easy to do. Some simply take a little longer than others, and as every busy host and hostess knows, time is of the essence. Therefore, the projects in this book are more or less presented in the order of the time needed to make them. And, believe it or not, the time can actually be measured in seconds, not minutes!

Every folded napkin in the book is suitable for paper and many can also be made with linen. If you use paper, it is advisable to use the heavier 3-ply; however, you will find most paper napkins are the softer 1-ply. If, in using the very soft paper, your productions tend to collapse, use two nap-kins together to give body. All of the folds in the book, however, were tested on 1-ply paper napkins, and they all worked.

If you use linen, it helps if you add some starch in the laundering. If you are still not able to make sharp enough creases where necessary, try a little spray starch, and they'll crease beautifully. When using linen, be sure to practice your folds first on paper napkins, so you won't spoil a freshly starched and ironed napkin. Then, when you start on the linen, you'll know exactly what to do. Special notes in each project tell you where linen is especially well suited for the folding.

Be sure after linen napkins are ironed flat that they are not put away folded or creased, so you won't have to re-iron before folding. In the case of paper napkins, the best way to get rid of the folds already in them is to run your fingernail *carefully* along the creases on the "mountain," or raised, side. This is also the easiest way to rip soft paper napkins, so do it very gently. Cloth, of course, should be ironed as flat as possible, especially on the edges.

You will find that paper napkins, because of the kind of soft, stretchy paper used to make them, rarely fold into perfectly lined-up squares, tri-angles, and so on; so, do not fuss over the initial folds. The napkins will come out looking better in the end than you might expect, even though the first folds might not be "true."

In the directions in this book, the fold you are to make is represented by a dotted line, and arrows show the direction of folding. The solid lines represent completed folds.

Some of the folded napkins are suitable for formal and semi-formal table service; others for informal, such as brunch, after-dinner coffee, casual teas, buffets, snacks. There are also folds that will liven up children's parties—such as the Sailboat, Elf's Shoe, Rabbit Ears or Flute. No matter what the occasion, you will find a unique and charming way to decorate your table with these festive folded napkins.

Illus. 1.

Fan

Fold (a) an open napkin double from bottom to top, and crease. Make another fold (a) from bottom to top. Make accordion pleats (b) from left to right. Depending upon the size of the napkin, make at least 6 pleats for a small one, 7 or 8, or more, for a larger napkin. Press pleats together firmly. Fan out the top (c) with one hand, holding the bottom pleats tightly together (c) with the other hand. Set on service plate (d). (If the Fan doesn't stand well enough to suit you, use two napkins together.)

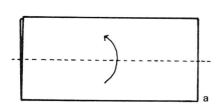

a

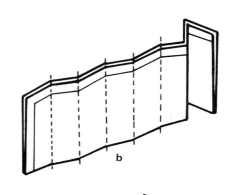

b

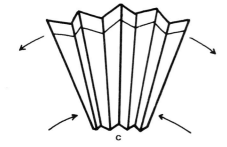

c

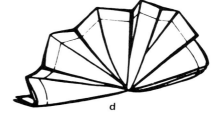

d

Japanese Fan

Fold (a) an open napkin double from bottom to top. Crease sharply. Make another fold (a) from bottom to top. Make as many accordion pleats (b) as you can from left to right. Press together tightly to crease. Open out (c). Pull each "valley," or indented area, down on one side (c), and then each valley on the other side (d). Press base together tightly and fan out at top (e) until napkin looks like (f). (See color Illus. 30.)

Illus. 2.

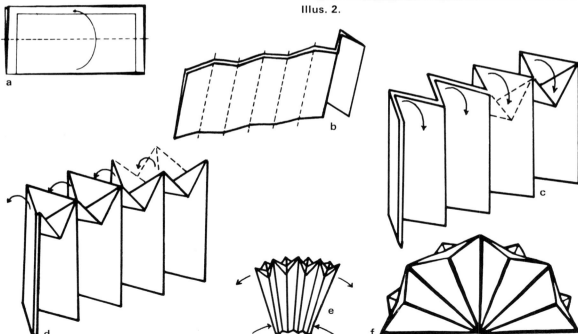

Double Japanese Fan

Use together two napkins of the same size, but different colors.

After first fold (a) from bottom to top, fold two halves, one on each side, down from top to bottom (a). Make tight accordion pleats (b). Press together. Pull out valleys on both sides (c) using two open-ended pleats only. Leave closed, middle-pleated part standing upright (c). Press base and fan out top (d). Finished napkin should look like (e) from both sides.

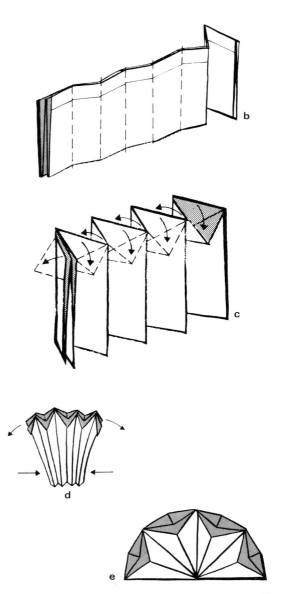

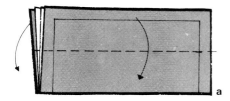

Illus. 3.

7

Festival

Fold (a) open napkin diagonally from one corner to opposite corner, forming a triangle (b). Beginning at closed base, accordion-pleat (b) the triangle until it looks like (c). Then fold (c) across the middle. Press flat. The napkin will naturally fall into the shape shown in (d) when placed on plate. Or, tuck one half under service plate as in Illus. 4.

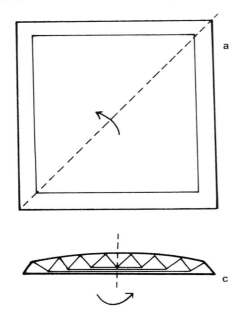

a

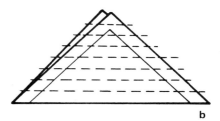

b

c

d

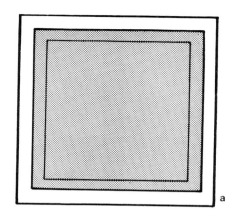

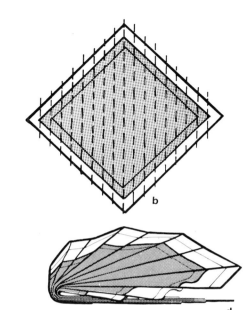

Illus. 5.

Double Festival

Use two different-colored and different-sized napkins, say a 16″ and a 13″.

Place the small napkin on large napkin (a) and accordion-pleat (b) together from one corner to the opposite. Make a fold (c) across the middle. Tuck one end under service plate and let other end fall gracefully across plate. (See color Illus. 34.)

Flute

Fold (a) napkin from one corner to opposite corner forming a triangle (b). Roll up (c) the triangle from wide base to top. Fold (d) roll across the middle, and press down to flatten slightly (e). Place on plate or upright in a glass.

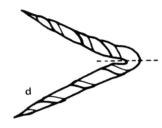

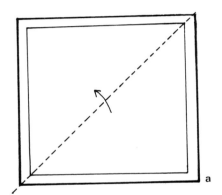

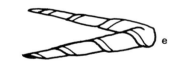

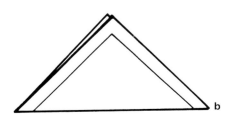

Double Flute

Use two napkins of the same size but different colors (Illus. 6).

Lay one on the other so that there is a $\frac{3}{4}''$ margin on two sides (a). Fold (a) from lower left to upper right corner. There should now be an equal

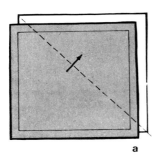

a

margin (b) on the two sides of the triangle. Roll (c) from wide base to point so that the napkin looks like a barber pole. Fold (d) across the middle and place in a glass. (See color Illus. 22.)

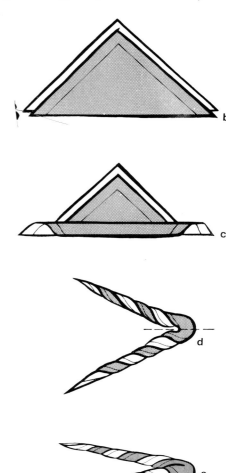

b

c

d

e

Illus. 6.

Blossom

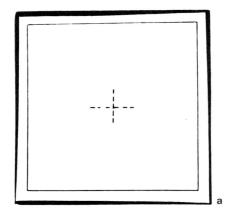

Illus. 7.

Suitable for either starched or unstarched linen, or paper napkins.

Open (a) a napkin full. Pick up (b) the napkin by the exact middle, and shake out. Run your other hand down the napkin, pressing the top 2″ together. Make a fold (c) and bend over. Insert folded end (d) into cup handle, between prongs of a fork, or under a service plate.

(See color Illus. 23.)

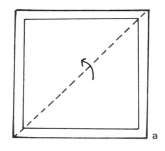

a

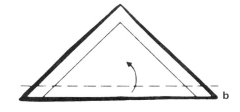

b

Illus. 8.

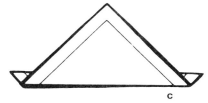

c

Candle

Fold (a) open napkin from one corner to opposite corner. Make one fold up (b) at base of the triangle. Turn napkin over (c). Roll up (d). Tuck end into the turned-up "collar" at the base. Pull down outside point at top (e). Stand next to glasses on table.

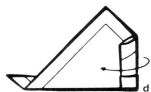

d

e

Sail

Illus. 9.

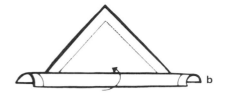

Suitable for linen or paper napkins.

Fold (a) napkin into triangle from bottom to top. Roll up (b) from bottom to within 2″ of the top. Fold (c) from right to left. Set upright (d) on plate. (See color Illus. 28.)

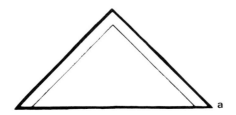

Sailboat

Fold (a) napkin twice to form ¼-size square, with open edges pointed down. Fold up (a) bottom point to meet top point. Fold in (b) sides to meet at the middle. Fold (c) bottom points back *under* and press flat. Fold back (d) napkin on the middle crease, so that it looks like (e). One by one, pull back (f) loose points so the napkin looks like (g).

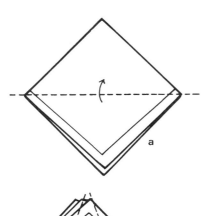

a

Illus. 10.

b

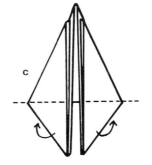

c

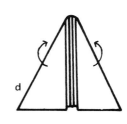

d

e

f

g

Butterfly

Open (a) a napkin fully. Accordion-pleat (a) the entire napkin, making quite narrow pleats (b). Make a fold (c) across the middle and twist (d) both ends. Fan (e) pleats out. (Can be inserted in cup handle before pleats are fanned out.)

(See color Illus. 31.)

Illus. 11.

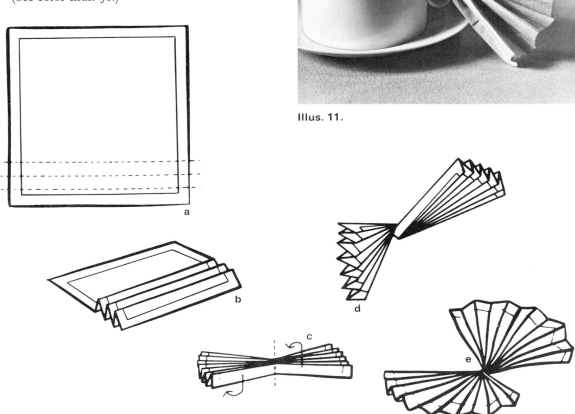

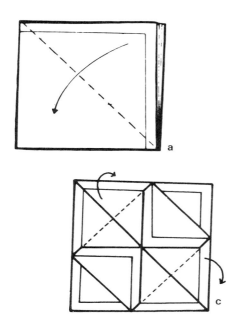

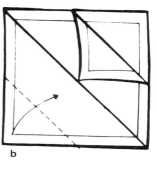

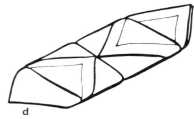

Triangles

Suitable for linen or paper napkins.

Fold (a) a napkin twice so that it is $\frac{1}{4}$-size, placing open edges on top and right side. Fold down (a) the top free corner at upper right to opposite corner at lower left. Fold (b) next top free corner just to the middle. Fold first corner back to meet second corner at the middle (b). Fold (c) other two corners *under* to meet in middle of back. Turn back over (d).

Illus. 12.

17

Wings

Illus. 13.

Suitable for paper or linen.

Fold (a) napkin in half from bottom to top. Fold (a) again from bottom to top. Make one large pleat (b) towards the middle from the left side, then (c) from the right side. *Roll* (d) top parts under as shown if using linen, or *fold* (e) under if using paper. Lift wings gently and place on plate.

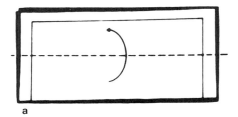

a

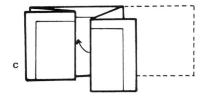

c

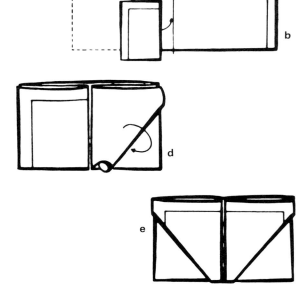

Bishop's Mitre

Fold (a) a napkin from bottom to top. Fold (a, b) left top corner down to the middle and lower right corner up to the middle. Make a fold (c) parallel to long sides and pull up the two points (1, 2) so they are not within the fold. Bend (d) one side round and tuck (e) into the other side. Bend (f) other side round and tuck (g).

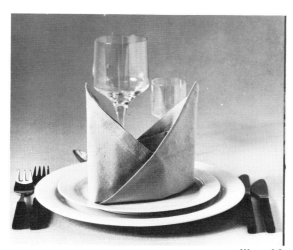

Illus. 14.

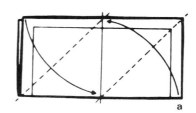

a

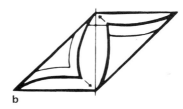

b

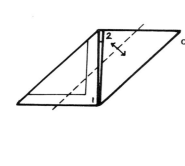

c

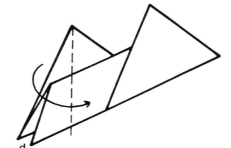

d

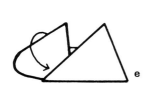

e

f

g

Spire

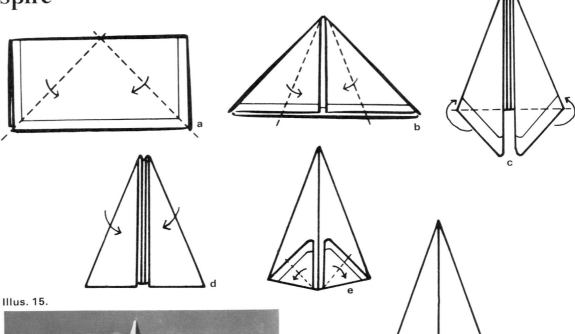

Illus. 15.

Fold (a) napkin over in half from top to bottom. Fold down (a) two top corners so they meet flush in the middle. Fold (b) two sides towards the middle again so the long sides meet. Fold (c) the two resulting points at the bottom towards the *back*. Fold (d) the napkin along the middle fold *towards* you, reversing the crease already there. Sharpen this crease. Pleat (e) the two projecting points at the base once each (Illus. 15).

Palm Leaf

Suitable for paper or large linen napkins.

Fold (a) double from bottom to top. Fold (a) a single upper corner towards the middle; then other single upper corner towards the middle. Turn the napkin over. Fold down (b) entire top edge flush with bottom. Lift right-hand corner of this folded-down part and turn up (c), keeping a finger on the middle of the napkin. Turn back (c); then turn back the other corner. Turn the napkin over again. It should look like (d). Press all creases sharply. Accordion-pleat (d) from right to left. Make sure that one pleated fold is exactly in the middle of the napkin, or it will not stand straight when fanned out (e).

Illus. 16.

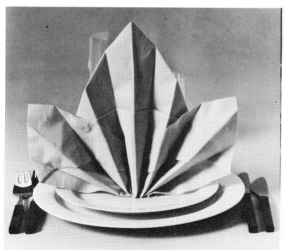

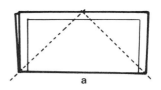

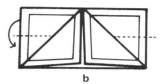

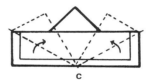

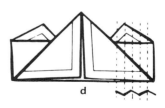

21

Swan

Fold (a) a napkin twice so it makes a ¼-size square. Have all open ends at top and on right side. Pull (a, b) one corner down and pleat (c) towards the middle. Pull another corner down and pleat (d) towards the middle so it lies next to the first pleat. Fold (d) napkin in the middle with pleats on top (e). (See color Illus. 27.)

Illus. 17.

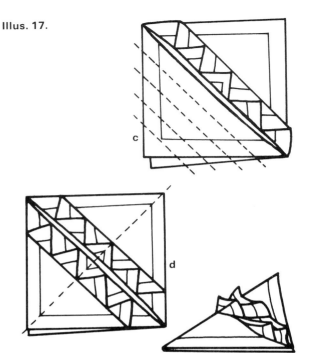

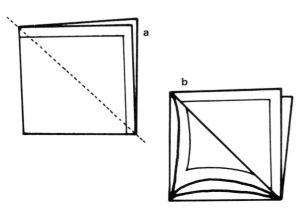

Double Swan

Use two different-colored, same-size napkins.

Fold (a) them together twice to make a ¼-size square, open edges at top and right side. Fold back (b) two free corners at upper right and pleat (c) them together towards the middle. Fold back two more free corners and pleat these together towards the middle so they lie alongside the first pleat (d). Fold (d) the napkin from corner to corner across

22

the pleats with the pleated parts on top. The Double Swan will stand upright on a plate (Illus. 18) if you bend it under (e) and fasten at the back (f) with a staple.

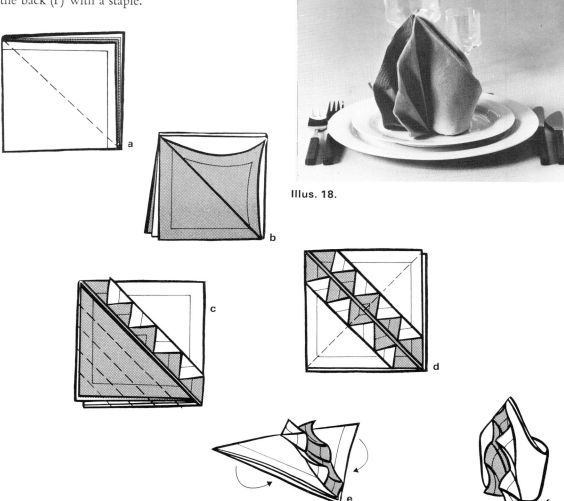

Illus. 18.

Illus. 19.

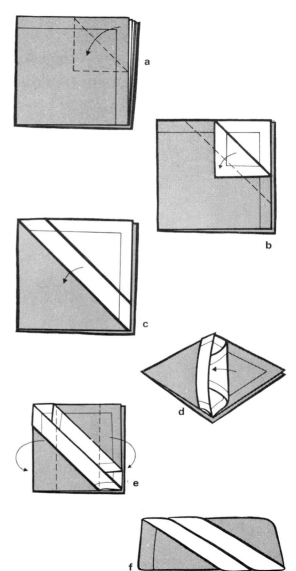

Buffet

Well suited to either linen or paper napkins.

This fold can be done with either a single napkin or two same-size, different-colored napkins, such as in Illus. 20. The instructions are for two napkins.

Fold (a) napkin twice into a $\frac{1}{4}$-size square, open edges on top and right side. Fold (a) down upper right corner in two thicknesses until the points are at the exact middle of the square (b). Fold (b, c) down twice more so that the napkin is cut by a diagonal. Fold (d) two more edges and tuck them into "pocket" at the middle. Fold (e) the two sides *under* so they meet in back. Place flatware inside the pocket.

Illus. 20. Buffet.

Fleur-de-lis

Illus. 21.

Fold (a) napkin from top to bottom and from corner to opposite corner. Fold (a) two upper corners down to meet in the middle, forming a square. Fold (b) the two turned-down points back up to meet at the top. Fold (c) bottom point up to meet the central edges. Turn up or fold (d) the lower part so that it overlaps the upper part at least $\frac{3}{4}''$, forming a collar around it (e). Bend (e, f) napkin from front to back and insert one point of the collar into the other to secure them together (g). Turn down (h) the two loose flaps and tuck (i) them into the collar.

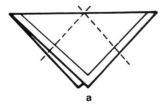

a

26

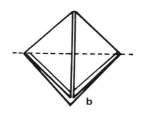

b

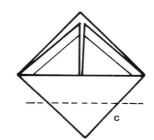

c

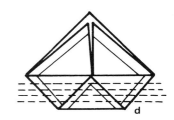

d

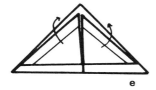

e

f

g

h

27

Illus. 22. Double Flute.

Illus. 23. Blossom.

Rocket

Illus. 24.

Fold (a) napkin in half from bottom to top. Fold again (a) from bottom to top. Fold (b) two sides down so they meet in the middle. Turn (c) napkin over. Roll (d) each flap outward. Fold (e) rolls up so they meet in the middle. The napkin will look like (f). Turn over (g) and place on plate.

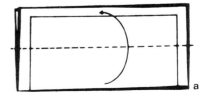

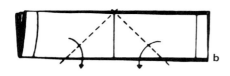

b

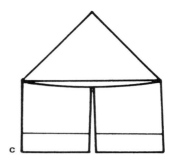

c

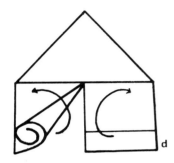

d

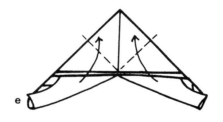

e

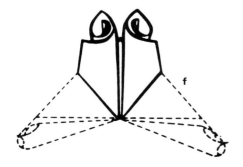

f

g

Illus. 25. Flower.

Flower

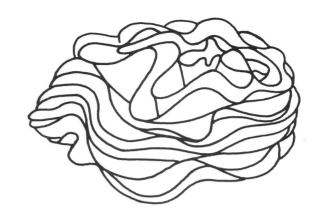

For paper napkins only.

Cut out at least a dozen squares, of whatever size you wish, from paper napkins in two or three colors. Stack them together and make a hole through the middle (a). Insert a brass fastener into the hole and fold it back to keep the sheets together. Fold (a) from corner to corner. Fold again (b) from side to side. Fold again (c) from side to side. Cut (d) the top edge to form a heart shape. Open flat and pull out (e) the sheets one by one to form the flower. The large flower in Illus. 25 can be made by using whole paper napkins opened out flat.

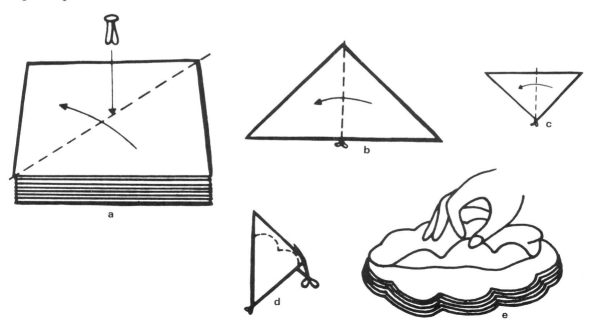

Rabbit Ears

Illus. 26.

Suitable for starched linen and paper napkins.

Fold (a) open napkin from bottom to top and top to bottom so the two parts overlap exactly, forming three equal parts. Fold down (b) both top corners to meet in the middle. Fold up (c) both bottom corners to meet in the middle. Fold in (d) two lower sides to meet in the middle to look like (e). Turn napkin *over* and *upside-down* to look like (f). Fold up (f) lower triangle. Fold (g) napkin back on both sides of the middle. Fasten with staple at back. Pull rabbit ears apart a little. Spread base slightly to sit on plate.

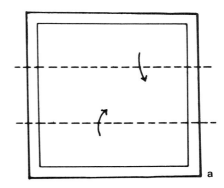

a

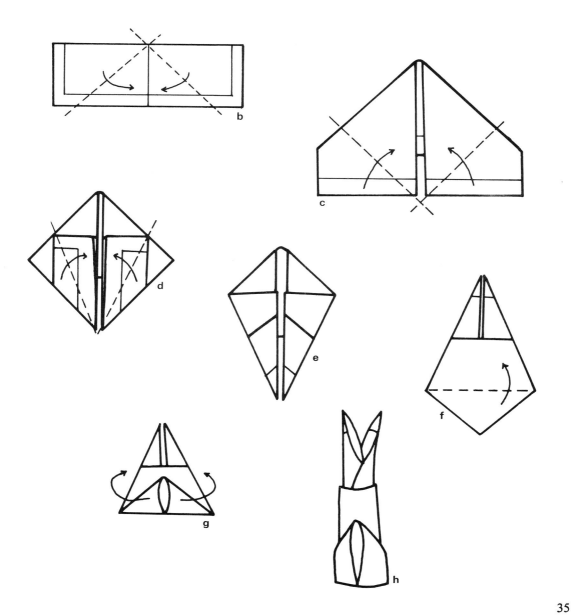

b

c

d

e

f

g

h

Illus. 27. Swan.

Illus. 28. Sail.

Elf's Shoe

Illus. 29.

Suitable for starched linen and paper napkins.

Fold (a) napkin from bottom to top twice. Fold down (b) upper corners to meet in the middle. Fold in (c) upper sides to meet at the middle. Fold (d) napkin down the middle. Hold in left hand in position shown in (e). Fold (e) "wing" nearest you up to left. Tuck (f) other "wing" into slitted opening. Turn toe up slightly (g).

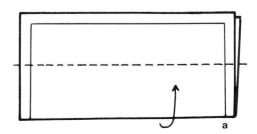

38

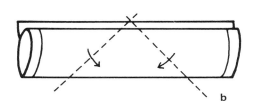

b

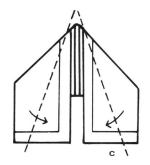

c

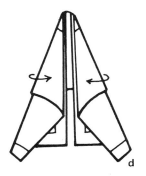

d

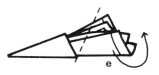

e

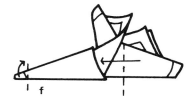

f

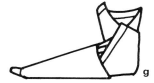

g

Illus. 30. Japanese Fan.

Illus. 31. Butterfly.

Princess

Make two accordion pleats (a), one from the top, and one from the bottom, so they meet exactly in the middle. Fold back (a) each pleat along the exact middle so three open edges are on top (b). Accordion-pleat once (b) from both sides to meet in the middle (c). Fold top flap (d) into a triangle and press hard to crease. Make triangles (e) with each flap by reversing crease in the middle of each pleat (f), resulting in (g).

(See color Illus. 33.)

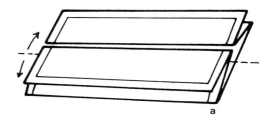

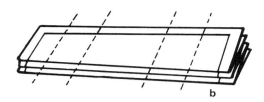

b

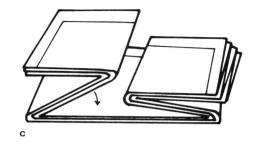

c

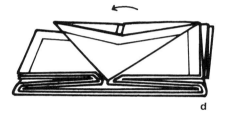

d

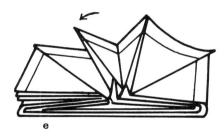

e

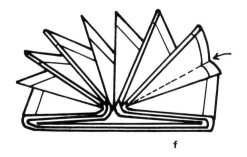

f

g

Illus. 33. Princess.

Illus. 34. Double Festival.

Water-Lily

Fold in (a) all four corners of an open napkin so they meet in the middle. Again fold in (b) all four new corners to join in the middle. Turn napkin over. Press flat. Fold up (c) corners to meet in the middle so it looks like (d). Press creases sharply. Hold in the middle with one hand, and, one by one, pull corner flaps on the underside up (e), punching in "mountain peaks," until all four corner flaps are up (f). Then pull single "leaf" parts up from underneath and fluff out (g). [Steps (e), (f), and (g) can also be done even more easily by placing (d) over a glass or cup before pulling.]

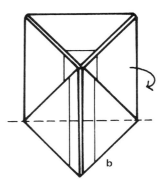

b

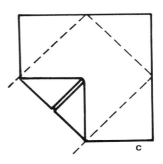

c

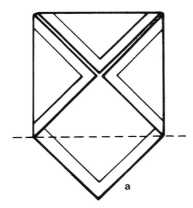

a

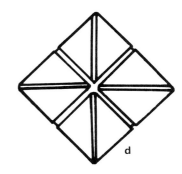

d

Illus. 35.

e

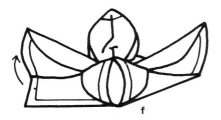

f

g

Flower Decoration

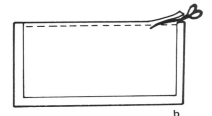

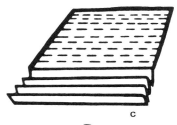

Illus. 36.

Fold (a) a *paper* napkin from top to bottom. Cut (b) along folded edge so there are two pieces. Accordion-pleat (c) from left to right. Tie (d) or tape round the middle lightly. Gently pull up (e) pleated layers one by one. Use two or more napkins together to achieve fuller flowers (f).